HAL LEONARD
GUITAR
TAB METHOD
SONGBOOK

To access audio visit:
www.halleonard.com/mylibrary

7523-8508-8633-6962

ISBN 978-1-4584-1640-7

HAL•LEONARD®
7777 W. BLUEMOUND RD. P.O. BOX 13819 MILWAUKEE, WI 53213

Visit Hal Leonard Online at
www.halleonard.com

TABLE OF CONTENTS

TABLE OF CONTENTS

All the Small Things

Words and Music by Tom De Longe and Mark Hoppus

Key of C

Intro

Moderately fast

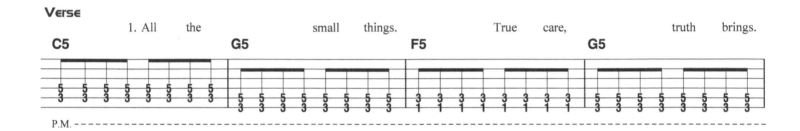

Verse

1. All   the   small   things.   True   care,   truth   brings.

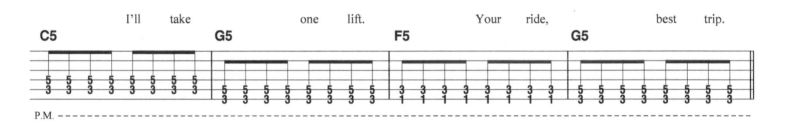

I'll   take   one   lift.   Your   ride,   best   trip.

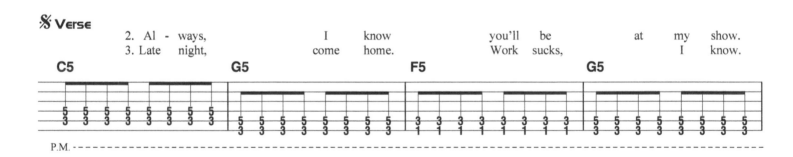

𝄇 Verse

2. Al - ways,   I   know   you'll   be   at   my   show.
3. Late   night,   come   home.   Work   sucks,   I   know.

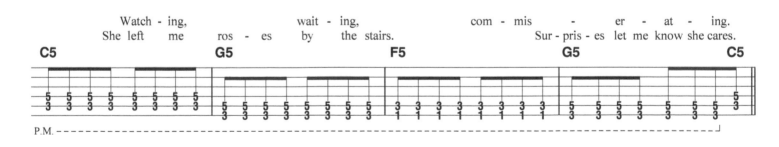

Watch - ing,   wait - ing,   com - mis - er - at - ing.
She   left   me   ros - es   by   the   stairs.   Sur - pris - es   let   me   know   she   cares.

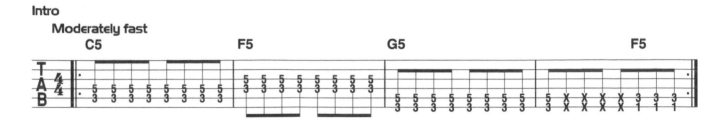

Pre-Chorus

Say   it   ain't   so.   I   will   not   go.   Turn   the   lights   off.   Carry   me

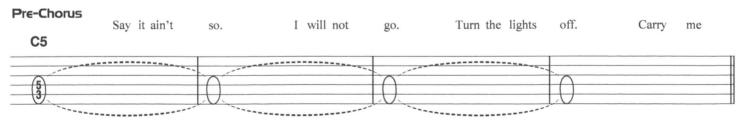

Chorus

home.
Na, na, na, na, na, na, na, na, na, na.   Na, na, na, na, na, na, na, na, na, na.

C5   G5   F5

To Coda ⊕

Na, na, na, na, na, na, na, na, na, na.   Na, na, na, na, na, na, na, na, na, na.

C5   G5   F5

Interlude

C5   F5   G5   F5

D.S. al Coda

C5   F5   G5   F5

⊕ **Coda**

mill. }   Say it ain't so.   I will not go.   Turn the lights off.   Carry me

C5   G5   F5

home.   Keep your head still.   I'll be your thrill.   The night will go on,   my little wind -

1.

C5   G5   F5

2.

on,   the night will go on,   my little wind - mill.

F5   C5

Breaking the Law

Words and Music by Glenn Tipton, Rob Halford and K.K. Downing

Key of A

Intro
Fast

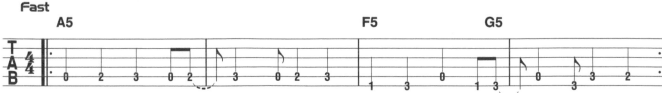

Verse

1. There I was, com-plete-ly wast-ing, out of work and down.

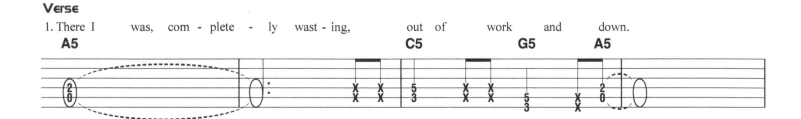

All in-side it's so frus-trat-ing as I drift from town to town.

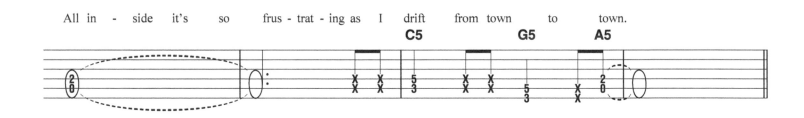

𝄉 Pre-Chorus

1. Feel as though no-bod-y cares if I live or die,
2. You don't know what it's like. You don't have a clue.

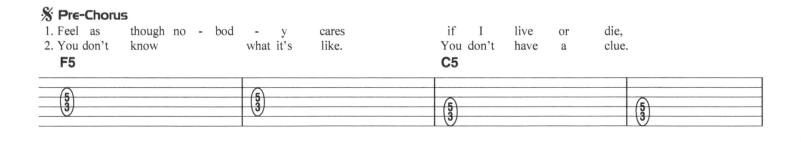

so I might as well be-gin to put some ac-tion in my life.
If you did, you'd find your-selves doing the same thing, too.

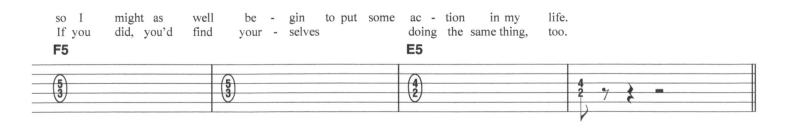

Chorus

Breaking the law,   breaking   the law.   Breaking the law,   breaking   the law.

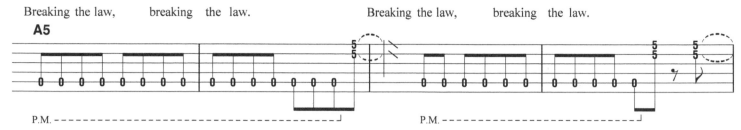

To Coda ⊕

Breaking the law,   breaking   the law.   Breaking the law,   breaking   the law.

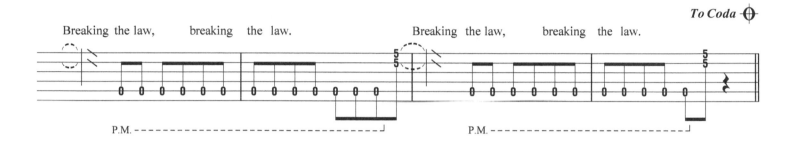

Verse

2. So much   for   the   gold - en   fu - ture,   I   can't   e - ven   start.

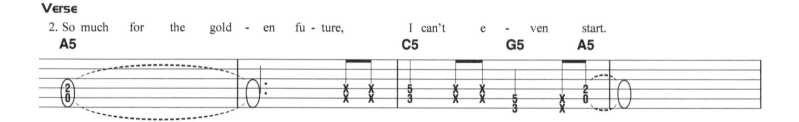

I've had   ev - 'ry   prom - ise   bro - ken,   there's   an - ger   in   my   heart.   *D.S. al Coda*

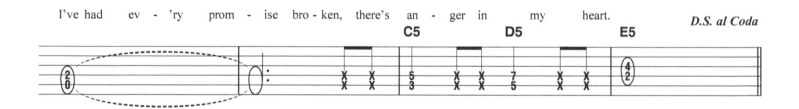

⊕ **Coda**

Breaking the law,   breaking   the law.   Breaking the law,   breaking   the law.

Play 3 times

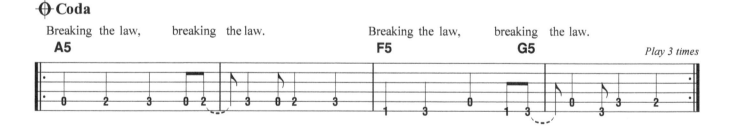

Breaking the law,   breaking   the law.   Breaking the law,   breaking   the law!

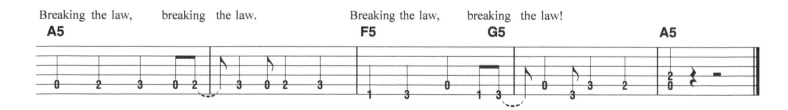

Californication

Words and Music by Anthony Kiedis, Flea, John Frusciante and Chad Smith

Key of Am

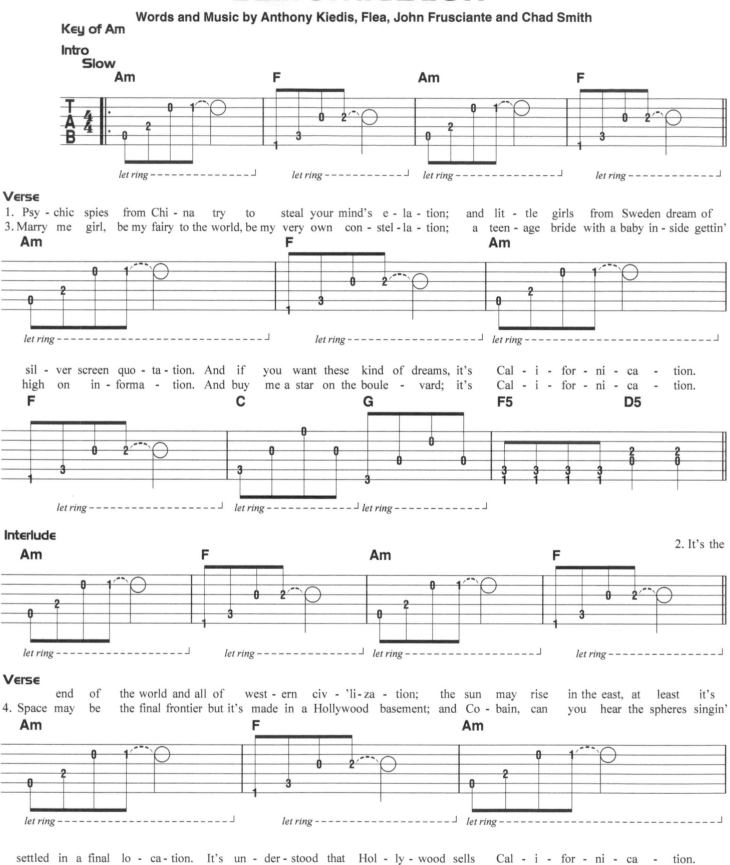

Verse

1. Psy - chic spies from Chi - na try to steal your mind's e - la - tion; and lit - tle girls from Sweden dream of
3. Marry me girl, be my fairy to the world, be my very own con - stel - la - tion; a teen - age bride with a baby in - side gettin'

sil - ver screen quo - ta - tion. And if you want these kind of dreams, it's Cal - i - for - ni - ca - tion.
high on in - forma - tion. And buy me a star on the boule - vard; it's Cal - i - for - ni - ca - tion.

Interlude

2. It's the

Verse

end of the world and all of west - ern civ - 'li - za - tion; the sun may rise in the east, at least it's
4. Space may be the final frontier but it's made in a Hollywood basement; and Co - bain, can you hear the spheres singin'

settled in a final lo - ca - tion. It's un - der - stood that Hol - ly - wood sells Cal - i - for - ni - ca - tion.
songs of station to sta - tion? And Al - der - on's not far a - way; it's Cal - i - for - ni - ca - tion.

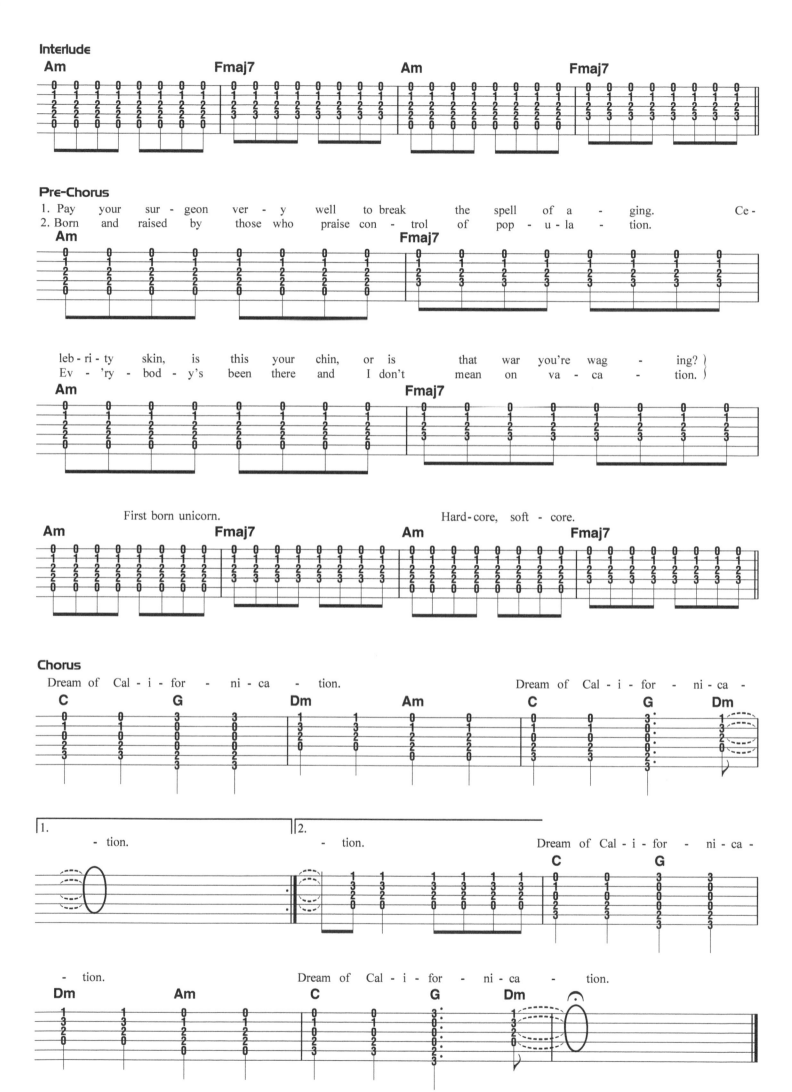

Come Together

Words and Music by John Lennon and Paul McCartney

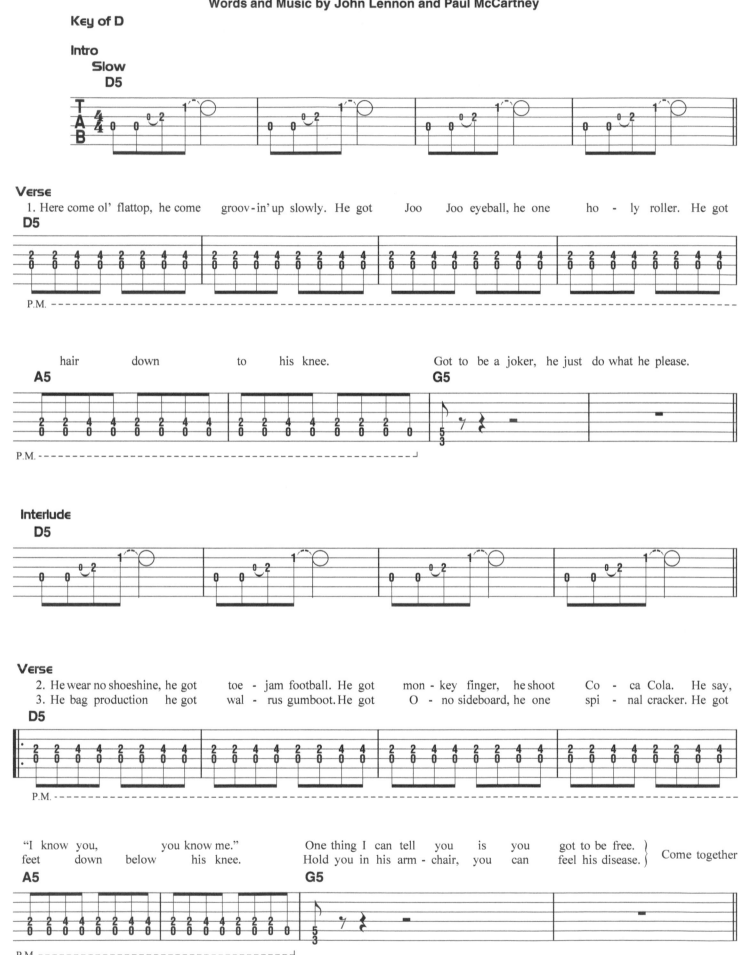

Chorus

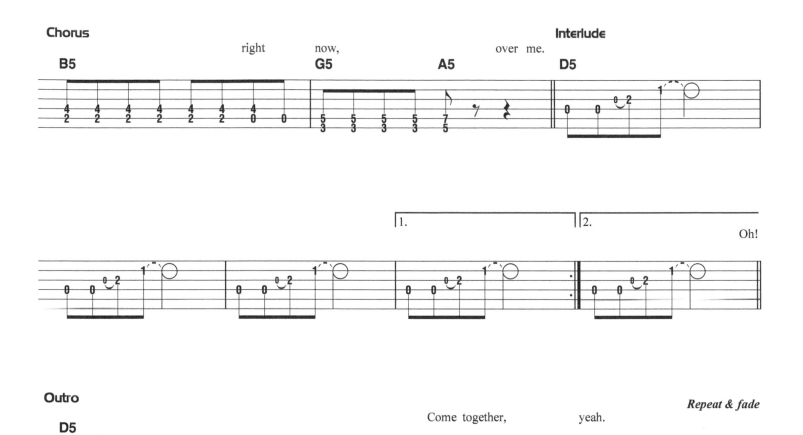

right   now,   over me.

Interlude

B5   G5   A5   D5

Outro

Repeat & fade

Come together,   yeah.

D5

Free Fallin'

Words and Music by Tom Petty and Jeff Lynne

Key of E

Intro

Moderately slow

1. She's a

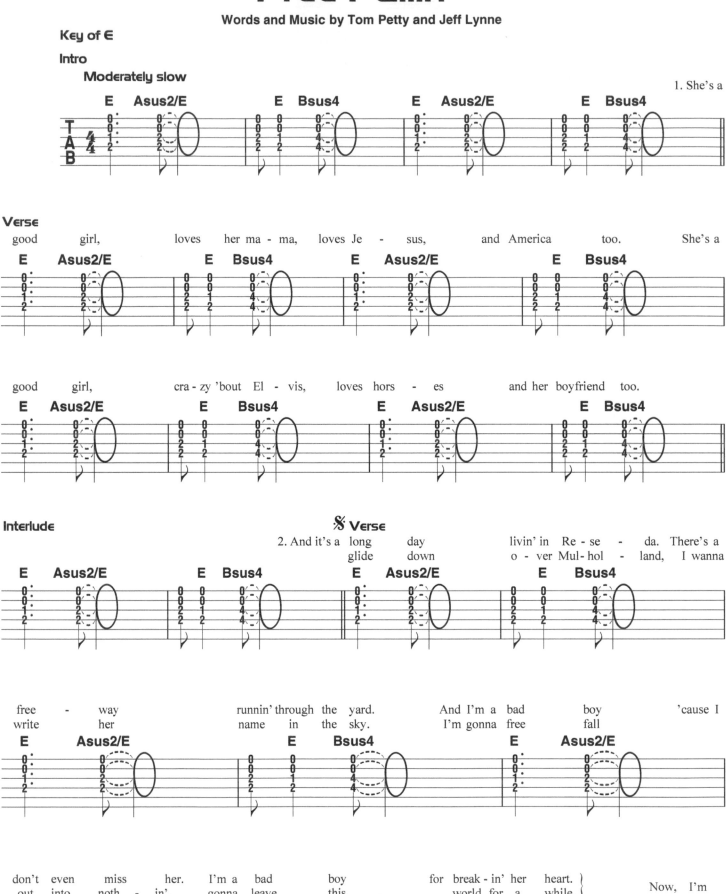

Verse

good girl, loves her ma - ma, loves Je - sus, and America too. She's a

good girl, cra - zy 'bout El - vis, loves hors - es and her boyfriend too.

Interlude   **%   Verse**

2. And it's a long day livin' in Re - se - da. There's a
glide down o - ver Mul - hol - land, I wanna

free - way runnin' through the yard. And I'm a bad boy 'cause I
write her name in the sky. I'm gonna free fall

don't even miss her. I'm a bad boy for break - in' her heart. } Now, I'm
out into noth - in', gonna leave this world for a while. }

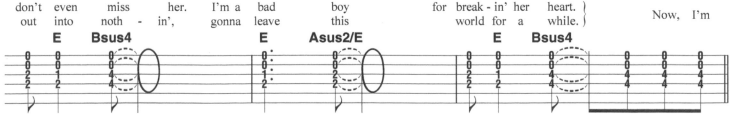

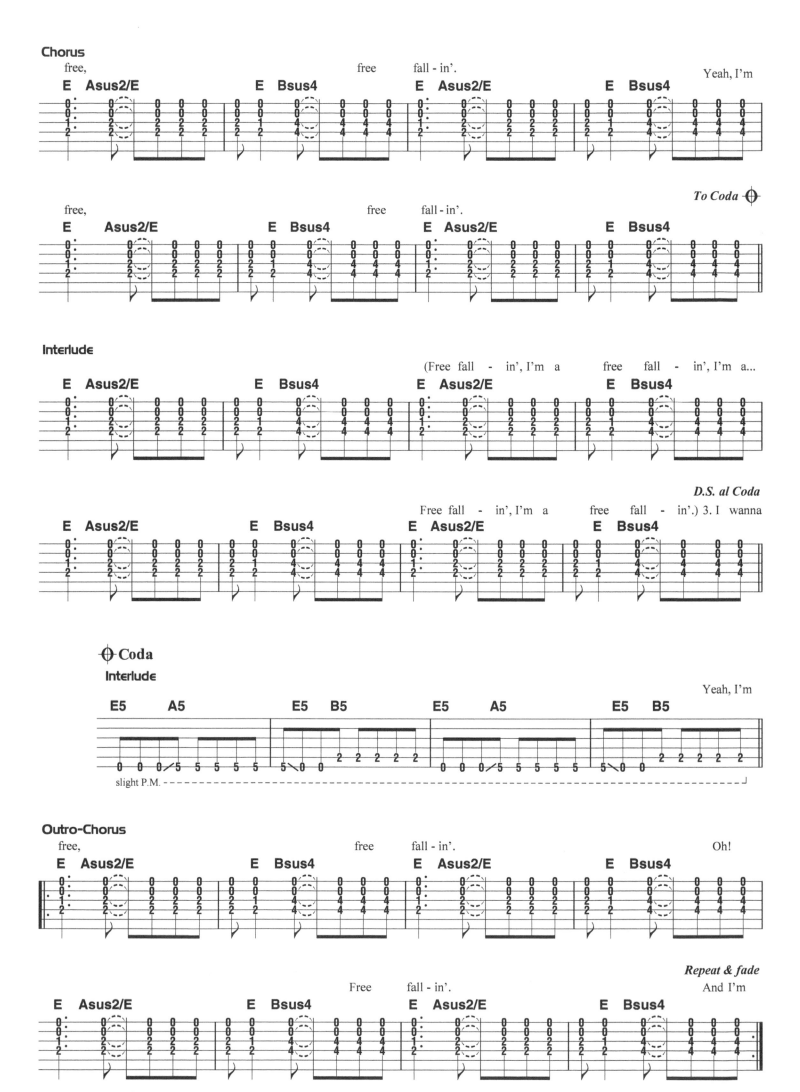

Lick It Up

Words and Music by Paul Stanley and Vincent Cusano

Key of A

Intro

Moderately

1. Yeah,   yeah.

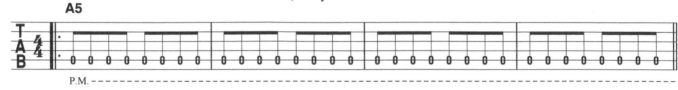

Verse

1. Don't wanna wait   till you know me   bet - ter.
2. Don't need to wait   for an in - vi - ta - tion.

Let's just be glad   for the time   to - geth - er.
You gotta live   like you're on   va - ca - tion.

Pre-Chorus

Life's such a   treat   and it's time you   taste it.
There's something   sweet   you can't buy with   mon - ey. Lick   it up.   Lick   it up.

There ain't no rea - son on   earth to waste it.)
It's all you need,   so be - lieve me, hon - ey.)   It ain't a crime   to be good to yourself.

Chorus

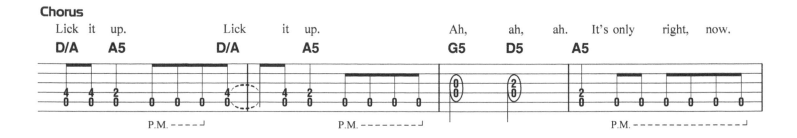

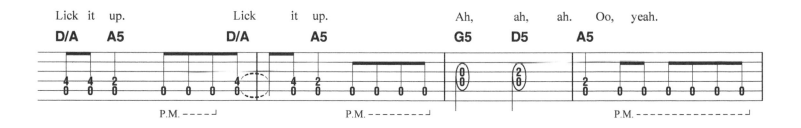

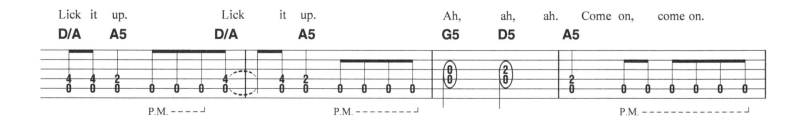

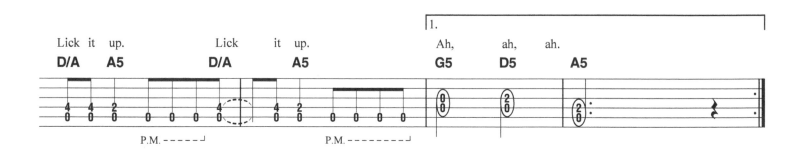

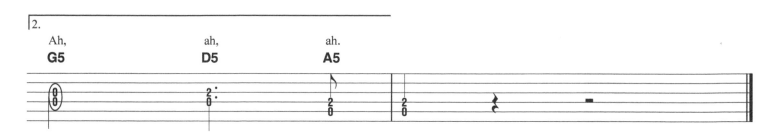

Pork and Beans

Words and Music by Rivers Cuomo

Key of G

Intro
Moderately
G

Verse

1. They say I need some Ro - gaine to put in my hair. (Mm, mm, mm, mm. Mm, mm, mm, mm.)
2. Ev - 'ry - one likes to dance to a happy song (Mm, mm, mm, mm. Mm, mm, mm.) with a

G

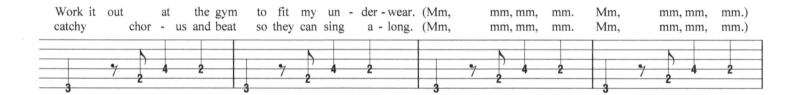

Work it out at the gym to fit my un - der - wear. (Mm, mm, mm, mm. Mm, mm, mm, mm.)
catchy chor - us and beat so they can sing a - long. (Mm, mm, mm, mm. Mm, mm, mm, mm.)

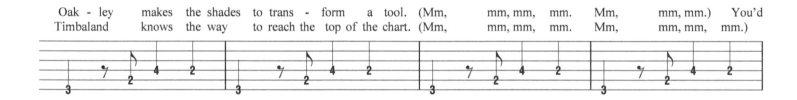

Oak - ley makes the shades to trans - form a tool. (Mm, mm, mm, mm. Mm, mm, mm.) You'd
Timbaland knows the way to reach the top of the chart. (Mm, mm, mm, mm. Mm, mm, mm, mm.)

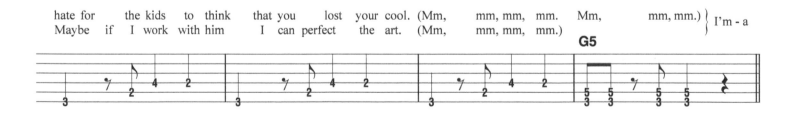

hate for the kids to think that you lost your cool. (Mm, mm, mm, mm. Mm, mm, mm.) } I'm - a
Maybe if I work with him I can perfect the art. (Mm, mm, mm, mm.)

G5

𝄋 Chorus

do the things that I wan - na do, I ain't got a thing to prove to you. I'll

G5   D5/A   E5/B   C5/G

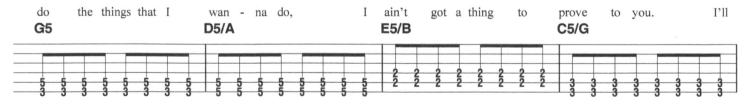

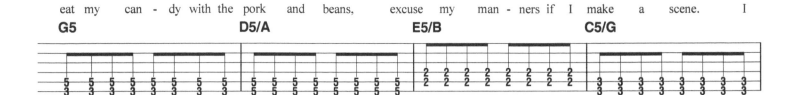

eat my can-dy with the pork and beans, excuse my man-ners if I make a scene. I

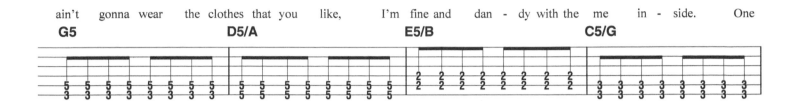

ain't gonna wear the clothes that you like, I'm fine and dan-dy with the me in-side. One

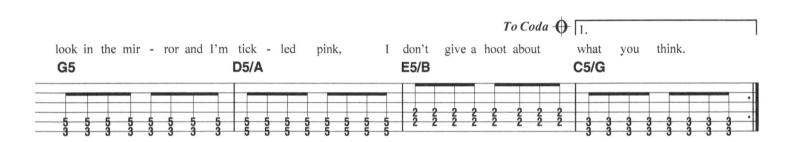

To Coda ⊕ | 1.

look in the mir-ror and I'm tick-led pink, I don't give a hoot about what you think.

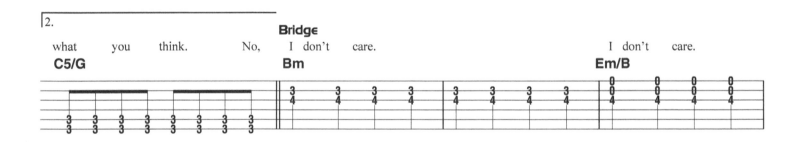

| 2.

what you think. No, I don't care. I don't care.

Bridge

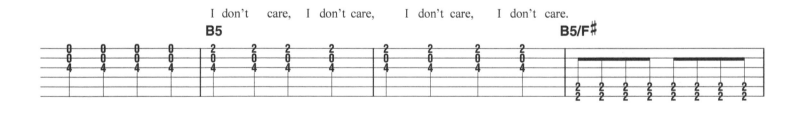

I don't care, I don't care, I don't care, I don't care.

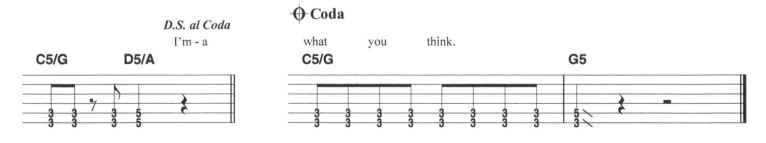

⊕ **Coda**

D.S. al Coda

I'm-a what you think.

17

Smells Like Teen Spirit

Words and Music by Kurt Cobain, Krist Novoselic and Dave Grohl

Key of Fm

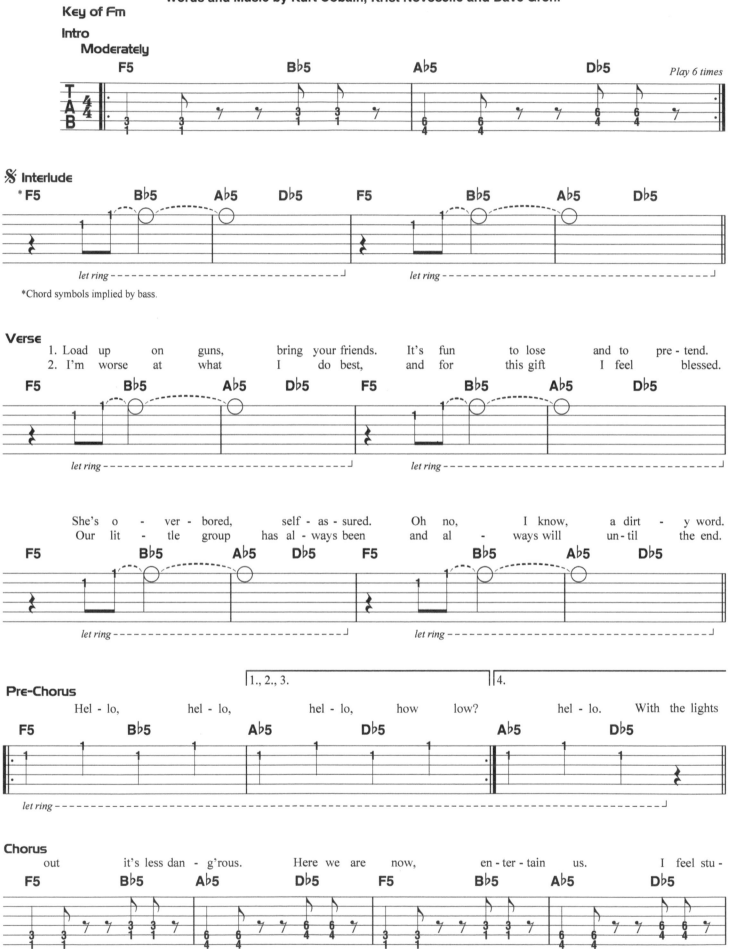

- pid	and con - ta - gious.		Here we are	now,	en - ter - tain	us.	A mul - la -
F5	Bb5	Ab5	Db5	F5	Bb5	Ab5	Db5

To Coda ⊕

- to,	an al - bi - no,		a mos-qui - to,		my li - bi - do.		Yeah.
F5	Bb5	Ab5	Db5	F5	Bb5	Ab5	Db5

Bridge

Hey.

F5	C/E	F5	Gb5		F5	C/E	F5	Bb5	A5	Ab5

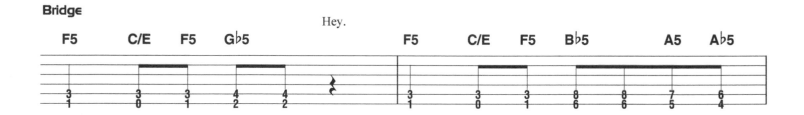

D.S. al Coda
(take repeats)

Yay.

F5	C/E	F5	Gb5		F5	C/E	F5	Bb5	A5	Ab5

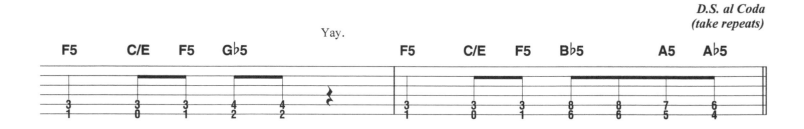

⊕ **Coda**

- do.	A de - ni - al,		a de - ni - al,		a de - ni - al!	
Ab5	Db5	F5	Bb5	Ab5	Db5	F5

Play 4 times

21 Guns

Words and Music by David Bowie, John Phillips, Billie Joe Armstrong, Mike Pritchard and Frank Wright

Key of G

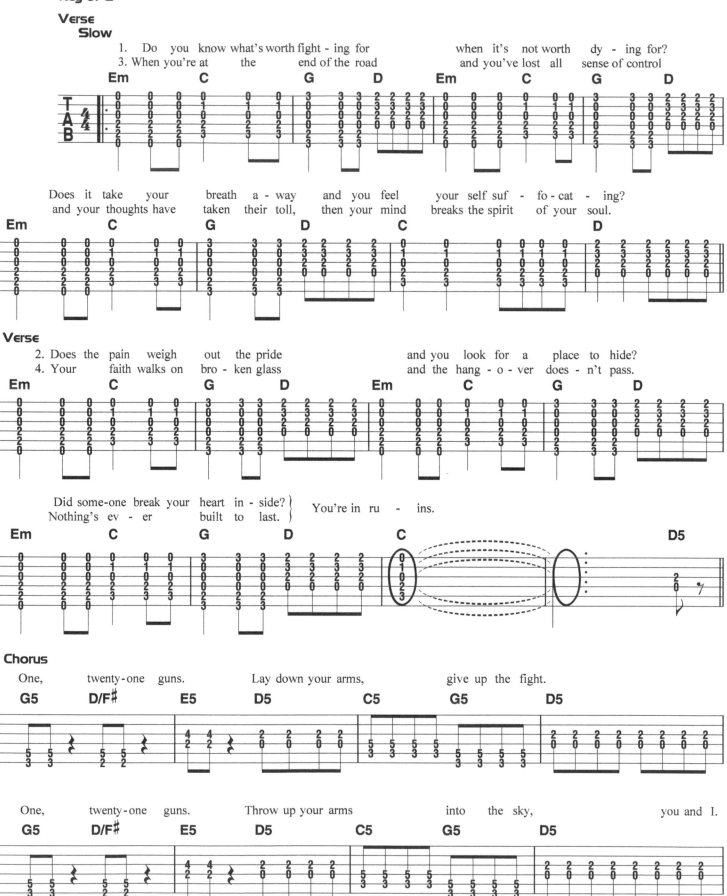

- contains samples of "All The Young Dudes" by David Bowie and "San Francisco (Be Sure To Wear Some Flowers In Your Hair)" by John Phillips

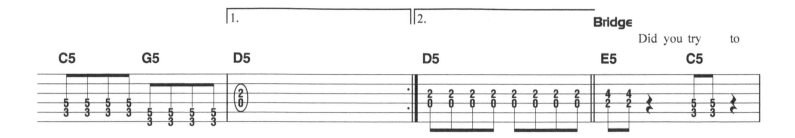

Bridge

Did you try to

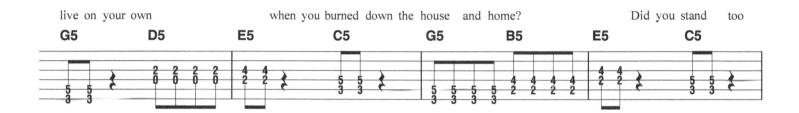

live on your own   when you burned down the house and home?   Did you stand too

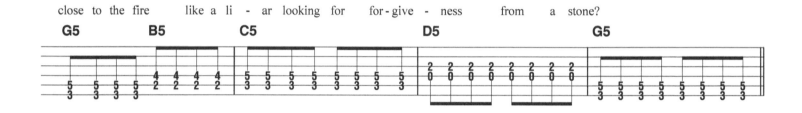

close to the fire   like a li - ar looking for   for-give - ness   from   a stone?

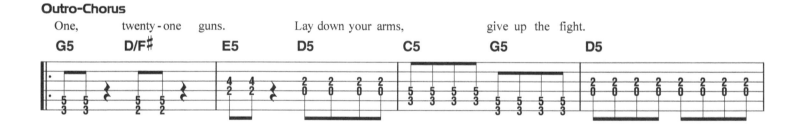

Outro-Chorus

One,   twenty - one   guns.   Lay down your arms,   give up the fight.

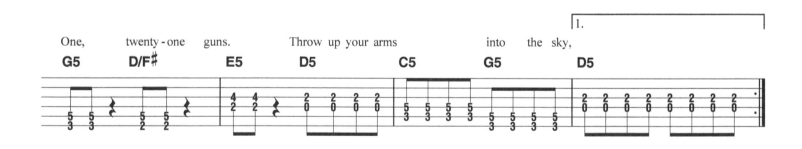

One,   twenty - one   guns.   Throw up your arms   into   the sky,

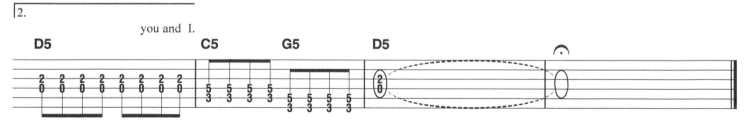

you and I.

You Really Got Me

Words and Music by Ray Davies

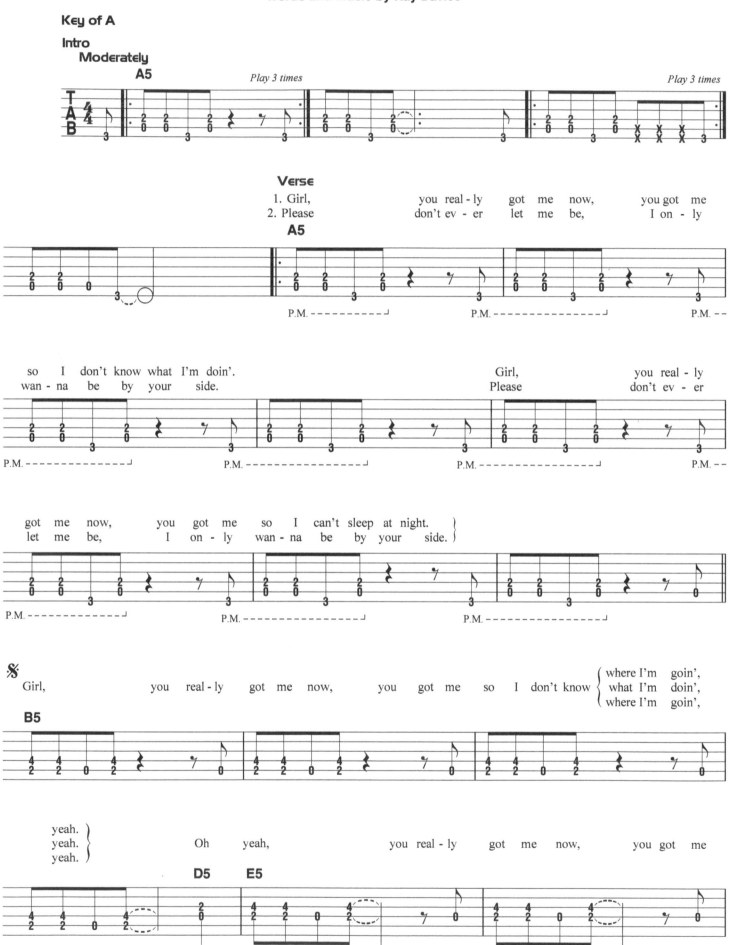

easy GUITAR play along

Audio Access Included

INCLUDES TAB

The *Easy Guitar Play Along* ® series features streamlined transcriptions of your favorite songs. Just follow the tab, listen to the audio to hear how the guitar should sound, and then play along using the backing tracks. Playback tools are provided for slowing down the tempo without changing pitch and looping challenging parts. The melody and lyrics are included in the book so that you can sing or simply follow along.

1. ROCK CLASSICS
Jailbreak • Living After Midnight • Mississippi Queen • Rocks Off • Runnin' Down a Dream • Smoke on the Water • Strutter • Up Around the Bend.
00702560 Book/CD Pack....... $14.99

2. ACOUSTIC TOP HITS
About a Girl • I'm Yours • The Lazy Song • The Scientist • 21 Guns • Upside Down • What I Got • Wonderwall.
00702569 Book/CD Pack....... $14.99

3. ROCK HITS
All the Small Things • Best of You • Brain Stew (The Godzilla Remix) • Californication • Island in the Sun • Plush • Smells Like Teen Spirit • Use Somebody.
00702570 Book/CD Pack....... $14.99

4. ROCK 'N' ROLL
Blue Suede Shoes • I Get Around • I'm a Believer • Jailhouse Rock • Oh, Pretty Woman • Peggy Sue • Runaway • Wake Up Little Susie.
00702572 Book/CD Pack $14.99

6. CHRISTMAS SONGS
Have Yourself a Merry Little Christmas • A Holly Jolly Christmas • The Little Drummer Boy • Run Rudolph Run • Santa Claus Is Comin' to Town • Silver and Gold • Sleigh Ride • Winter Wonderland.
00101879 Book/CD Pack......... $14.99

7. BLUES SONGS FOR BEGINNERS
Come On (Part 1) • Double Trouble • Gangster of Love • I'm Ready • Let Me Love You Baby • Mary Had a Little Lamb • San-Ho-Zay • T-Bone Shuffle.
00103235 Book/
      Online Audio..........$17.99

9. ROCK SONGS FOR BEGINNERS
Are You Gonna Be My Girl • Buddy Holly • Everybody Hurts • In Bloom • Otherside • The Rock Show • Santa Monica • When I Come Around.
00103255 Book/CD Pack.....$14.99

10. GREEN DAY
Basket Case • Boulevard of Broken Dreams • Good Riddance (Time of Your Life) • Holiday • Longview • 21 Guns • Wake Me up When September Ends • When I Come Around.
00122322 Book/
      Online Audio $16.99

11. NIRVANA
All Apologies • Come As You Are • Heart Shaped Box • Lake of Fire • Lithium • The Man Who Sold the World • Rape Me • Smells Like Teen Spirit.
00122325 Book/
      Online Audio $17.99

13. AC/DC
Back in Black • Dirty Deeds Done Dirt Cheap • For Those About to Rock (We Salute You) • Hells Bells • Highway to Hell • Rock and Roll Ain't Noise Pollution • T.N.T. • You Shook Me All Night Long.
14042895 Book/
      Online Audio........ $17.99

14. JIMI HENDRIX – SMASH HITS
All Along the Watchtower • Can You See Me • Crosstown Traffic • Fire • Foxey Lady • Hey Joe • Manic Depression • Purple Haze • Red House • Remember • Stone Free • The Wind Cries Mary.
00130591 Book/
      Online Audio........$24.99

HAL•LEONARD®
www.halleonard.com

Prices, contents, and availability subject to change without notice.